Victor Burgin Susan Hiller Calum Colvin Erasmus Schroeter Philip-Lorca diCorcia Sarah Jones
Simon Norfolk John Askew Anne Kathrin Greiner Minka Jakerson Jung Lee Gina Glover
Salvatore Arancio Paul Thomas Martina Mullaney Mark Durden Stella Santacatterina
Amanda Hopkinson Morgan Falconer Simon Morrissey Roy Exley Jeremy Millar Shirley Read

Erasmus Schroeter, Komparsen Frau V, *2000*

portfolio

the catalogue of contemporary
photography in britain

Erasmus Schroeter, Komparsen, *Frau II, 2000*

Victor Burgin has used the iconography of landscape to reflect upon the construction of national identities in two video installations being exhibited this autumn. *Listen to Britain*, made following his return to England after the events of September 11, draws on films produced in Britain during the second world war and makes reference to a conservative and idealised image of the nation at a time of anxiety and fear in the West. A timely counterpoint is his earlier video work, *Watergate*, which incorporates imagery of the American Romantic Painting Gallery at the Corcoran Museum in Washington DC, to reflect upon American history and power.

Also in this issue, Stella Santacatterina discusses the work of Susan Hiller, an artist who creates artworks which identify the ways in which vision is connected to knowledge, imagination and dreaming.

Some of the strongest work produced during 2002 on photography, film and fine art degree courses in the UK is represented in this issue by an international group of graduates: Anne Kathrin Greiner, Minka Jakerson, Jung Lee, Salvatore Arancio, Martina Mullaney and Paul Thomas.

Gina Glover, *Outside Time, 2002*

Susan Hiller, *From India to the Planet Mars, 1998*

Philip-Lorca diCorcia, *Head #01*

number 36 december 2002

Published in June and December by Portfolio Photography Workshop (Edinburgh) Limited
43 Candlemaker Row, Edinburgh EH1 2QB, UK
Tel (44) 0131 220 1911
Fax (44) 0131 226 4287

Email info@portfoliocatalogue.com

www.portfoliocatalogue.com

Inside Front Cover Erasmus Schroeter, Komparsen Frau XXI, 2001

subscriptions

United Kingdom
Individuals £34 for 4 issues / £18 for 2 issues
Institutions, Libraries and Colleges
£45 for 4 issues / £25 for 2 issues
Europe £45 for 4 issues / £25 for 2 issues
Worldwide Air £55 for 4 issues / £30 for 2 issues

distribution

UK Museum and Gallery Bookshops:
PORTFOLIO, 43 Candlemaker Row
Edinburgh EH1 2QB, UK
Tel (44) 0131 220 1911 Fax (44) 0131 226 4287

retail
Art Data, 12 Bell Industrial Estate
50 Cunnington Street, London W4 5HB
Tel (44) 0208 747 1061
Fax (44) 0208 742 2319
Email gold@artdata.co.uk
www.artdata.co.uk

reviews and essays

Simon Norfolk, *Afghanistan, 2002*

Anne Kathrin Greiner, *Disciplined Spaces, 2002*

Calum Colvin, *Ossian: Fragment I, 2002*

Victor Burgin, *Watergate (detail), 2000*

Sarah Jones, *The Fence (Passion Flower) (I) 2002*

Editor **Gloria Chalmers**

Subscriptions and Sales **Elizabeth Pardoe**

Design Consultants **Tayburn Corporate**

Design **Patricia Bartie**

Set in Foundry Sans **The Foundry**, London

ISSN 1354-4446

Scottish **Arts** Council
LOTTERY FUNDED

Funded by
THE
ARTS
COUNCIL
OF ENGLAND

·EDINBVRGH·
THE CITY OF EDINBURGH COUNCIL

Erasmus Schroeter
Komparsen (Bit-Part Player)

Frau I

Frau IV *(opposite)*

Frau II

Frau IXX *(opposite)*

Philip-Lorca diCorcia
Heads

Head #01

Head #03 (opposite)

Head #10

Head #23 *(opposite)*

Victor Burgin
Watergate, *video installation with sound*

I have an appointment with Peter at four o'clock.

I arrive at the café a quarter of an hour late. Peter is always on time. Will he have waited for me?

I look at the room and I say, 'He is not here.'

Is there an intuition of the absence of Peter, or does the negation come only with judgement?

At first sight it seems absurd to speak of intuition here, since there cannot be an intuition of nothing, and since the absence of Peter is precisely this nothing.

Everyday language, however, bears witness to this intuition. Do we not say, for example, 'I saw right away that he was not there'?

It is certain that the cafe itself is a fullness of being – with its tables, its booths, its mirrors, its light, its smoky atmosphere, and the sounds of voices, rattling saucers and footsteps that fill it. And all the intuitions of detail I can have are filled by these odors, these sounds, these colors. Similarly, the actual presence of Peter in a place I do not know is also a fullness of being.

It seems that we find fullness everywhere. But we must observe that, in perception, there is always the construction of a figure on a ground. No object, no group of objects, is especially suited to be organized as either ground or figure: it all depends on the direction of my attention. When I enter this cafe, to look for Peter, all the objects in the cafe are synthetically organised as the ground against which Peter is given as having to appear. And this organization of the cafe as ground is a first nihilation. Each

element of the room - person, table, chair - tries to isolate itself, to lift itself upon the ground constituted by the totality of other objects, only to fall back again into the indifferentiation of this ground, to be diluted in this ground. For the ground is that which is seen only as superfluous, as the object of a purely marginal attention.

So this first nihilation of all the figures, which appear and are swallowed up in the total equivalence of a ground, is the necessary condition for the appearance of the principal figure, which is here the person of Peter. And this nihilation is given to my intuition, I am witness to the successive fading of all the objects that I look at - especially the faces, which detain me for an instant ('Could that be Peter?') but which as quickly go out of focus precisely because they 'are not' the face of Peter. If, nevertheless, I should

at last discover Peter, my intuition would be filled by a solid element. I would be suddenly fascinated by his face and all the café would organize itself around him.

But Peter is not here.

This does not mean that I discover his absence in some precise place in the establishment. For Peter is absent from all of the café. His absence freezes the café in its fading. The cafe remains ground, it persists in offering itself as an undifferentiated totality to my only marginal attention, it slides in the background, it pursues its nihilation.

But it only makes itself ground for a determinate figure, a figure it carries everywhere in front of it, that it presents to me everywhere; and this

figure, which slips constantly between my look and the solid and real objects of the café, is precisely a perpetual fading; it is Peter raising himself as nothingness against the ground of nihilation of the café.

So that what is offered to the intuition is a fluttering of nothingness: the nothingness of the ground, the nihilation of which summons and demands the appearance of the figure, and that of the figure - nothingness which slides as a nothing on the surface of the ground.

This is what serves as foundation for the judgement…

Ruins of the Parthenon
1880
Sanford Robinson Gifford
American

View of Marshfield
1865-70
Martin Johnson Heade
American

Tamaca Palms
1854
Frederic Edwin Church
American

The Greek Slave
1846
Hiram Powers
American

Mount Corcoran
1876-77
Albert Bierstadt
American

Niagara
1857
Frederic Edwin Church
American

The Last of the Buffalo
1888
Albert Bierstadt
American

The Sun Vow
1905
Hermon A. MacNeil
American

Lacrosse Playing among the Sioux Indians
1851
Seth Eastman
American

The Departure
1837
Thomas Cole
American

The Return
1837
Thomas Cole
American

Endymion
1874
William Rinehart
American

Listen to Britain, *video installation with sound*

Cut to close-up of head of girl looking out of frame right.
She turns head towards centre to look directly out of frame above line of camera's look.

She turns her head left, still looking slightly up, then abruptly swivels head and shoulders through
near-180 degrees to turn her back to the camera and look out of frame left.

Simon Norfolk
Afghanistan

The old terminal for Jalalabad-Kabul buses

A government building close to the former Presidential palace at Darulaman, destroyed in fighting between Rabbani and the Hazaras in the early 1990s *(opposite)*

The district of Afshas in western Kabul. This Hazara neighbourhood was completely devastated during ethnic fighting between the residents and Rabbani's forces in the early 1990s.

The Shur Bazaar district of Kabul, destroyed by long-range rocket attacks between warring Mujaheddin factions in 1994 *(opposite)*

John Askew
Flower

Susan Hiller
From India to the Planet Mars

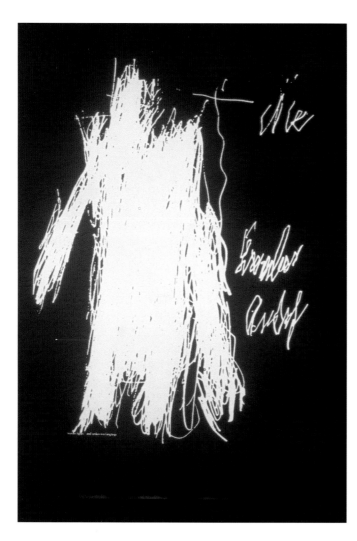

Calum Colvin
Ossian: Fragments of Ancient Poetry

Scota I *(above)*, Blind Ossian *(opposite)*

Overleaf: Fragment I *(left)*, Fragment VI *(right)*

Anne Kathrin Greiner
Disciplined Spaces: Aspects of Three German Schools

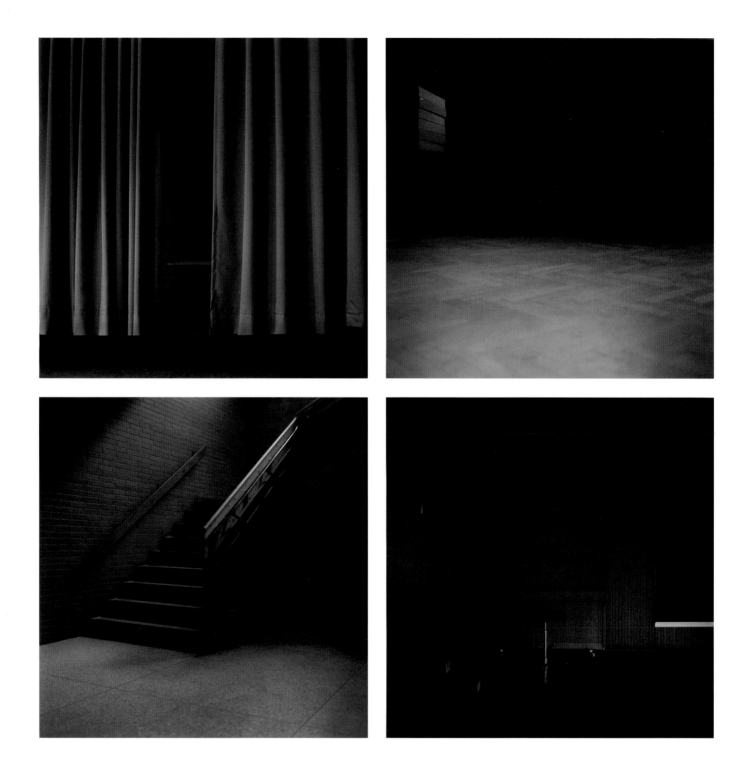

Grundschule Lützelsachsen, 1982-1986 (2002) *(and opposite)*

Dietrich-Bonhoeffer-Gymnasium, 1993-1995 (2002) *(and opposite)*

Minka Jakerson
The Yearning Room

Film Stills, 2002

Jung Lee
Clubgenki

Sarah Jones

The Park (I), 2002

The Rose Gardens (orange) (I), 2002 *(opposite)*

The Fence (Passion Flower) (II), 2002

The Fence (Passion Flower) (I), 2002 *(opposite)*

Martina Mullaney
Turn In

Salvatore Arancio
The Ballroom Dancers

Paul Thomas
Sauna

pilgrims who walked the ancient hillside to Canterbury. It is caught up in the mysticism at the core of the film, centred on the quasi-diabolical figure, Colpepper, a Justice of the Peace, archaeologist and gentleman farmer, who it also turns out, is the glue man, pouring glue in local girls' hair to stop them going out with American servicemen at night. Burgin makes reference to this aspect of the film through a short text presented as a dissolve accompanied by the music of Benjamin Britten. The reference to the glue man serves to disrupt the idyll of landscape imagery. It gives an air of threat and menace, which we might also invest in the action of the young woman in the fragment from Powell and Pressburger's film. Though there are no signs of fear, her repeated gesture begins to signal some agitation and unease, that sense of threat which Burgin identified with the nation on his return to an England alert to potential terrorist attacks.

Listen to Britain rests upon a dialectic between the enigmatic and haunting presence of the young woman and the lush landscape shots. One landscape view of fields and hills has a sense of foreboding, since a storm cloud hovers overhead. This view, both still and moving, is accompanied by a soundtrack fragment from *A Canterbury Tale*, in which a woman is talking about the view – from the same hillside Burgin filmed his landscape – and how she spent the happiest days of her life there in a caravan with her fiancé, who is now missing, feared dead. The extract reiterates the sense of magic and spirit attached to the landscape as she wonders if the soul of her absent fiancé lives on in this beautiful setting. Her conversation also raises the spectre of class as she tells her male companion how her fiancé's father never approved of the relationship believing his son could do better than a 'shop girl'. It would need an earthquake, she says, to change him, to which her companion replies, "We're having one".

Burgin's reflections on Englishness at a time of threat through citations of fictional moments from film, recall his repetitive use of an extraordinary fragment from Duvivier's *Pépé le Moko*, made in the 1930s, in both his video pieces, *Venise* and *Remembering/Repeating*. Burgin replays and slows down the moment when Jean Gabin, running through the Casbah after the woman he loves, stumbles and falls down. As he falls a woman in purdah can be seen rising. This charged fragment, as Norman Bryson has pointed out can be seen as a "fast forward replay of French Colonial history, from 19th Century Orientalism through to the independence movements of recent history."[3] In the video installation of *Remembering/Repeating*, a screen showing Jean Gabin's stumble and fall was set against another showing the multi-ethnic crowds filmed by Burgin on the moving walkway at the Montparnasse metro station, the site of recent Islamicist terrorist attacks.

If questions about Englishness, the countryside and national identity are raised by *Listen to Britain*, Burgin's *Watergate*, 2000, a single screen video projection currently on show at Matt's Gallery, reflects upon American history, power and corruption. A slow panoramic sweep takes the viewer repeatedly around a room in Washington's Corcoran Museum showing 19th century American landscape paintings and sculpture. On the soundtrack a woman reads a passage from Jean-Paul Sartre's *Being and Nothingness* talking about going into a café and looking for someone who has left, a phenomenological reflection on the persistent presence of those who aren't there. The camera then takes us around a hotel room overlooking offices where the Watergate scandal took place. The two spaces are connected through the painting of Frederic Edwin Church's *Niagara*, the original which hangs in the gallery and a reproduction of which hangs in the hotel. A title sequence derived from the labels of the American

paintings and sculptures follows, accompanied by an aria from one of Handel's Cantatas. *Watergate's* formal structure is fluid, with the continuous turning of the panoramic view, digitized from a series of still images. *Listen to Britain* as a looped succession of fragments, bits of film and soundtrack snippets, is formally more fractured and disruptive.

The panoramic gaze implies a totalising, omnipotent vision, yet what is revealed in *Watergate* is far from this. Instead, the work reflects upon versions of America's past, on one hand the cultural history and authority bestowed on the nation's artistic treasures and on the other, through the hotel window's view – which framed by the hotel window echoes and links up with the framed landscapes in the Corcoran Museum and the framed reproduction image of Niagara on the hotel wall – buildings which serve as a reminder of political cover-up and corruption, the scandal which haunts the American present just as Sartre is haunted by the person whom he missed at the café. If the official sanctioned sense of an American history might be gleaned by the authority of the state's display of artworks in the Corcoran, the scandal of Watergate offers us the other side of its history. Burgin's repetitive insistence on the Corcoran's display of paintings and sculpture, moving round and round the walls of the museum and the listing of the artworks' labels – giving titles, dates and the names of the artists and their nationality, all American – begins to unsettle any sense of a seamless history in this collection. The iconography of the art in the Corcoran in its very heterogeneity – the mock Classical white marble figures, *The Greek Slave* and *Endymion*; the portrayal of American Indians in the sculpture, *The Sun Vow*; and paintings showing, as the titles indicate, such subjects as *The Ruins of the Parthenon*, *The Last of the Buffalo*, *Lacrosse Playing Among the Sioux Indians* – highlights the construction of American identity through cultural appropriation. This display of paintings and sculpture from the past makes us think about America's hegemony in the present, its assimilation and erasure of other cultures.

What *Watergate* has in common with *Listen to Britain* is the use of the iconography of landscape scenery to reflect upon and raise questions about the formation and construction of national identities. Such video works, sensuous, enigmatic, affective and formally compelling, continue the interplay between psychic and social realities integral to Victor Burgin's series of elliptical photo texts from the 1980s. And now the resonance and allusions are broader and more wide-ranging through the medium of video, creating a more malleable and multi-sensory form which one gets the sense is closer to the processes of the dreamwork.

1. Interview with Peter Suchin, *Dpict*, Dec/Jan 2000-01, p.38.

2. This and subsequent quotes taken from Burgin's comments on Listen to Britain in 'Where to Begin?' in Catsou Roberts, *Relocating*, August Media / Arnolfini, 2002, p. 146.

3. Norman Bryson, 'Victor Burgin and The Optical Unconscious' in *Victor Burgin*, Barcelona: Fundacio Antoni Tapies, 2001, p. 45.

Listen to Britain, video installation with sound *(detail)*, 2002

Susan Hiller
Anamorphosis of the Gaze

STELLA SANTACATTERINA

Psi Girls, 1999

"Muses are like women who slip out during the night when no one is looking and give themselves to unknown sailors, then return and speak about Chinese porcelain."

W.B.Yeats

Susan Hiller's work occupies an original and anticipatory place with respect to the landscape of contemporary international art, drawing on many cultural references, from anthropology to psychoanalysis to mass media technologies, and operating across various means from photography to installation, sound and object. It presents a continuity of aesthetic experience that the artist began in the early 1970s through an exploration of the deep place of visibility using complex and poetic minimal means. Marcel Proust might have said that her work is an astonishing revelation of the "mysterious phenomenon of scintillation", meaning that it searches for the secret source of artistic creation and the place of its realisation.

Her work pays particular attention to the way vision is connected to the dynamics of remembrance, knowledge, imagination and dream, with all the signs of the unconscious and the archetypes of collective memory. If the phenomenological world is a catalogue of statistics, the fantasy of the artist confronts the false surface of appearances to insert the invisible energies of the imagination, an exorbitant and poetic dimension, touching the poles of the disturbing and amazing. The imagination, says Foucault, is not in fact the way of reality; instead it is the realm of the actual, a means to traverse obliquely concrete presence in order to make the primal dimension emerge. In this respect all Hiller's work is 'work in progress', a circular tension of interrogation, oscillating between the presence of the question and the absence of the answer.

Psi Girls is an installation of five simultaneous video projections, each a montage of brief sequences from various popular films that figure an act of telekinesis performed by young girls. For instance, among them we recognise the shots in which a girl's powers of concentration alone spins a pencil on its point (Andrew Fleming's

The Craft, 1996) or accelerates a miniature train around a track (Brian de Palma's *The Fury*, 1978) or shifts glasses across a table to smash out of frame onto the floor (Andrei Tarkovsky's *Stalker*, 1979). Each screen is suffused by a different colour, altering the nature of the images and remapping their semantic meanings: violet and the sacred, green and the supernatural, blue and regeneration, yellow and transgression, red and passion. Of the six primary colours, orange, now thought by psychologists to reflect internal harmony, is 'missing'. The projections are accompanied by a pulsating soundtrack remixed from a gospel choir, which contributes to a sense of disorientation and amazement. Roger Caillois speaks of such disorientation as one of the most important keys of the mythical 'figure': "and yet, to this disorientation is linked the sense of vertigo and the pleasure to destroy order and stability." Indeed Hiller's work is always orchestrated around nuances of the occult and the aberrant, the play of the vertiginous, and a ludic panic that confuses us to produce a disjunction with established reality.

This disjunction is both external to the work in its relation to the viewer, and internal in its choice of themes. *Wild Talents*, 1998, juxtaposes documentary footage about a miraculous visionary appearance and religious pilgrimage, with the destructive psychokinetic power of children as projected through the images of mass media. This destruction of order is accentuated by the soundtrack of breaking objects, so that what is witnessed by the spectator has a double value: on the one hand it is understood as a representation, but on the other it is experienced as real. As in *Psi Girls*, Hiller creates a journey that activates a dynamic that works to defeat any certainty of the visible, developing an intentional disequilibrium of knowledge. In this respect, the artist operates a kind of language parallel to science where she manipulates suspicion and doubt to pass beyond established conventions. Her work deals with a phantasmatic internal world, but this world relies also, in Hegelian terms, on a series of transformations which are able to exteriorise the work. Art needs and is nourished by ghosts, but at the same time gives itself through a work of transformation, an anticipation of the final result. In this weaving the journey of potentiality multiplies and creates a constant shift of meanings into other possible constructions.

All Hiller's artistic practice is crossed and penetrated by memory and nostalgia, which nonetheless belong to the same horizon: representations of images that are distant, lost or denied, which emerge from oblivion. Like the historical example of the Surrealists, the concept of mourning in Hiller's work affirms itself almost as an intrinsic quality of the language of art itself. And yet nostalgia for the lost disorder underlines the new order of form. It is born from conscious awareness of art and of its contrary, the unconscious; in other words, born from the ambivalence of each gesture, because it is exactly ambivalence that gives the gesture a real affect through the presence in it of vital affirmation and mortal negation. There is no nostalgia, in fact, that is not remembrance; the myth of Mnemosyne can stand for both memory and nostalgia. Mnemosyne is the daughter of sky and earth, of Uranus and Gaia; in other words, the daughter of the visible and the invisible, from the past and the present. The birth of Mnemosyne describes a tension that moves beyond the border, but also challenges a spatial and temporal limit. The language of art is always marked by this presence; the link of art with memory is not therefore a casual relation but is inscribed in its roots, in its essence. Nostalgia, when it becomes the language of art, always elaborates itself as ambivalence, as does memory, producing an image that always comes back from a distant time and place, a movement of thought towards what is behind, lost, discarded – a distance that breaks the rules of the irreversible and impossible.

In both *Wild Talents*, 1998, and *Psi Girls*, 1999, the artist's mode of operation is similar to the analytic aesthetic of Godard, who constructed a mechanism capable of triggering the self-reflective and critical aspect of the filmic as well as the televisual image. His process was to slow down and deconstruct the flux of the image and treat each frame as if it were a photographic image. Especially in *Psi Girls*, where the artist uses five monitors, the new narrative shifts temporality from the linearity and succession of conventional film to the direct immediacy of the event more typical of TV, or even theatre. We are still voyeurs, but we are captured by the moment.

Hiller understands that the photographic image, despite its privilege as a seemingly pure registration of the material world, is nonetheless an oblique eye capable of reflecting things, but in a modified way. In *From India to the Planet Mars*, 1998, Hiller

demonstrates how this registration is no longer a language parallel to drawing or writing, or even to the readymade, but rather a completely different alphabet. *From India to the Planet Mars*, a series of illuminated photo-transparencies of obscure calligraphies, takes its title from a book by Theodore Flournoy (Switzerland, 1899) based on messages written automatically by Helen Smith which, according to her, represented the language of Mars and India. Hiller's drawings derive from not only the artist herself but also other sources (students and friends as well as Dr Anita Muhul's *Approaches to the Unconscious*, Harper's *George Yeats: On the Making of Yeats' 'A Vision'*, 1987, and Andre Breton's *The Automatic Message*, 1933). This is also a work in progress, in which the transparency takes on the qualities of both drawing and photograph, and where the illuminated gesture refers back to the experience of writing itself. But it is a deceptive linguistic process, a displacement from drawing to positive-to-negative transparency, whose deep meaning lies in its reference to an action that has already happened but which alludes to the real experience of the artist. It is the awareness of a subject that controls the flow of time and her own individual presence, but that also enables the viewer to recompose the work by connecting his or her own individual memory and temporal dimension. As in most of Hiller's works, *From India to the Planet Mars* alludes to the possibility of a journey, which is nostalgic not in the sense of a regressive return, but rather of the elastic capacity of memory for infinite extension, from which art draws and brings back a new poignancy to the culture of the present.

Dream Screens, 2000, is a work designed for late-night web-browsers (to be found in the Dia Center's website). It is constructed around the artists' colour wheel (here in the form of a web), dissolving fields of colour and a collection of whispered narratives based on dreams articulated against three background sounds: pulsar, Morse code and heartbeat. Light and energy are amongst the greatest mysteries of our time, and colour has much to do with this, since it is always in the interstices of things, invading everything, and yet remaining to be domesticated. Colour – extremely mobile, gradable – comes, like the pulsar, from the furthest place, which is also the unthinkable. The *horror vacui* indicates the loss of self and is linked to the still point, the other *par excellence*, but this infinite distance between subject and object is the original place from which aesthetic sensibility emerges.

As Nietzsche commented, "we need all the petulant, fluctuating,

From India to the Planet Mars, 1998 *(installation)*

dancing, derisive, childlike and beatific air in order not to lose the freedom over things that are idealistically demanded from us." Freedom is not a value outside temporality, but rather a continuous, tangential meeting with the world that happens outside the symmetrical movement of reason. Imagination here is neither conceived as an onanistic exercise on the possibility of the world nor as an allegorical emphasis on the simple interiority of the artist, but as an integral functionality uncontaminated by exteriority. From here, the intriguing and uncanny images the artist produces are founded in an optical play of anamorphosis, a perspective construction that makes strange things happen magically, pushing narrative meaning towards paradox and contradiction. As with the anamorphic figure in Holbein's painting *The Ambassadors*, the gaze carries a warning that disorder comes from order, and that a tormented world can result from the most rigorous organisation. Anamorphosis is a mechanical process, the logical but deformed consequence of perspectival optics, and links with the cold technological media Hiller uses. In her work there is a continuous exchange between margin and significance in which the fertile zone is the margin.

Fully aware of the irremediable linguistic nature of art, the artist articulates her work from this margin, or zero-degree of meaning, tending towards the transitivity of the language of art. This means that the work moves around the web of the imagination beyond the narrow confines of the psychology of the subject. Hiller's images carry the memory of the imagination itself, but as with language, the imagination must go beyond the self to belong fully to contemporaneity. Furthermore, this artistic attitude confirms a will to create a change within artistic structure, but above all a revolution at the level of art's meaning, to take into account an external referent, expressing a need for history and action as well as fantasy (and in this sense Hiller is a 'European' artist). In her case we can speak about art as a double gaze: one is external, incorporating the image of the world whilst transforming it; the other is an act of deviation, a transverse and circular practice

belonging to fantasy. This fantastic activity can neither be influenced by the symbolic decodification of psychoanalysis nor by a search for motivation in the artist's ego, but by an imagination that projects itself to the exterior in order to transform it.

Hiller's practice is a revitalisation of creativity that links both to the imagination and the irrational. In this respect the work shows a singular critique of both our culture and art. If we consider the condition of contemporary aesthetic research where there is a tendency to privilege the rational and the material over the spiritual, magical and mythic, Hiller's work demonstrates the necessity of art to rescue aspects of the mythopoetic, the imagination and the irrational. This does not mean to go against reason, but rather to recuperate mythic possibility. Therefore her attitude is different to that of the Surrealists since, although she cultivates the occult and oneiric, it is never for the dream in itself. Her artistic practice realises not so much objects as conceptual journeys in which the viewer can once again travel. This journey is always exercised within the boundary of ritual to confirm the field of absolute knowledge. Ritual becomes the moment capable of bringing art into a mythical place. The artist traces the moment of ritual through image, sound and words that become a catalogue of the genesis of artistic creation.

The experience of automatic writing, in Hiller's work, which first appeared in *Sisters of Menon*, 1972, and continues through *From India to the Planet Mars* and the telekinetic powers described in *Psi Girls*, is very close to Blanchot's idea of writing, where art is an adventure in which the artist loses herself. This adventure paradoxically becomes a fertile migration, going beyond the extreme limit of what no longer has any limit. Art is a space deprived of subjectivity: to draw, to write, demands the evacuation of the ego because only when the world becomes invisible can the event of art be born. For Blanchot, "blindness is the poetic space of vision"; for Heidegger, for a work of art to be 'successful' it must completely negate the person and the name of the poet, evoking the spoken in its pure state. In other words, the object of art is without subject.

Psi Girls, 1999 *(installation)*

A Scottish World-Theatre
Calum Colvin's Ossian

DAVID ALAN MELLOR

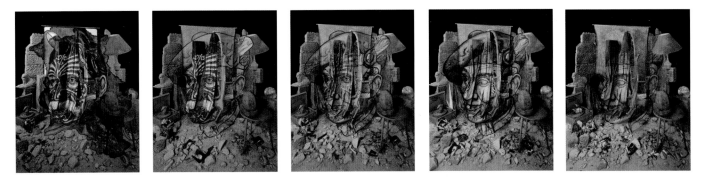

From the series Fragments I – VIII, 2002

What Calum Colvin has drawn up, in the eccentric dioramas of this exhibition, are twilight scenes of ruin. As such they are part of the larger narrative of Colvin's photographs of the last two decades, where broken visions have proliferated through the agency of perverse perspectives and disrupted micro-architectures. But his *Ossian* group, exhibited at The Scottish National Portrait Gallery in Edinburgh this autumn, have the kind of extensive cultural, national and historical specificity to them which always seemed promised, but always lay latent in Colvin's work. Now his extended theme of ruin focuses upon Scotland, or rather a series of literary and historical constructions of Scotland, from the 18th and 19th centuries. These are constructions which take on a precarious monumental appearance, but whose monumentality – to the current spectator – perpetually dissolves into oblivion. This process of dissolution occurs as a series of steps across the series *Blind Ossian I-IX* and *Fragments I-VIII* ; a sequence of collapsing correlatives for the fate of James McPherson's ur-text of Gaelic culture, *Fragments of Ancient Poetry Collected in the Highlands of Scotland*, published in 1760 and sensationally exposed as a fabrication by Dr. Johnson 15 years later.

The historical ruin of this narrative returns, under Colvin's manipulations, as a baleful theatre, where Ossian himself fixes us reproachfully rather than ecstatically, in his dead stare. He fades into a stone backdrop where an orange afterglow of history is kindled amongst the occluding Pictish stones in *Blind Ossian VIII* and *IX* . This massive but ghostly patriarch – McPherson's invented Ossian – was presented to the cultured elites of the still new Great Britain and Europe, as the Gaelic equivalent of Homer. So Colvin extends that aspect of blindness attributed to Homer to his conjured portrait of Ossian, producing a truly uncanny gaze. Oracular territory: a bedrocked script of a gaunt, stony, primal Scotland, like the melancholic *Scota*, who dreams those discontinuous pictures which might compose her as "...the shattered fantasy of the... lost organic society that haunted the western imagination."[1] The personified and Primitivist Scota, augmented and assailed by tokens of advanced digital technology, is kin to that diagrammatised Maori which Colvin outlines in the first two photographs from the *Fragments* set, transposed from a drawing by an English artist in New Zealand, traced with a full scientific anthropological fervour, in a careful cartography of Primitivisation.

This depicted, multi-textualised, foundationality is a piece of spectacular, but shaky, theatre or cinema. Colvin composes a flickering comic melodrama of origins, a suspect set of dissolving images (like the transformation of Dr Jekyll into Mr Hyde), a process which Colvin demonstrates in his digitisation of runic writing in *Scota*, morphing it and shuffling it from Pictish mark to replica of an oil portrait of McPherson by Sir Joshua Reynolds. These mutable historical signs and their technological vehicles – Colvin mimics heavily varnished 18th century oil on canvas in the making of these photographs – dwell on all the resonances of fabrication. One implication is that the project of archaically writing Scotland through a fabricated text falls apart like the ruined visual structures which inhabit the photographs. The counterfeiting of (national) culture is reduced to a barely perceptible trace – that trope of fading which runs through the entire exhibition. The reticulated tattoo/fingerprint whorls which adorn the face of the Maori and fade into the face of Harry Lauder in the *Fragments* series become a counter-contour and camouflage which breaks the Doric Pictish space of the *Blind Ossian* series, too, finally disappearing into the contingent hewings on the dressed stone.

Ultimately, in *Fragments VI* , *VII* and *VIII*, the Scots pomp projected on curtains, screen and scenographic stage, is slashed and endures a pyroclastic fate – like the streets of Pompeii or Lower Manhattan – of dust and shards. Especially dust: the picture-producing relic of the Aldis slide projector, which takes up its position to the right downstage of the *Fragments* series, has definitely lain defunct on a college technician's shelf for more than 25 years. Yet it can still be revived, still signal and perform its commanding office like the British Naval Aldis Lamp. Colvin has it project a sliver of that warm orange glow, that nostalgic 18th century light, sourced out of Claude, which the Hanoverian landscapists deployed, that empire of light which beams internally out of the turning globe in *Fragments*.

To a close and attentive eye, the Aldis projector's slide holder frames angled vignettes from another layer of fictional Scottish identities: stills from *Brigadoon*. But they are un-illuminated and like the dead eyes of Ossian himself, these emblems are dull and sombre, since the sun has set on this episode of Imperial transformation-scene and all but an ashen lunar light is present, like the lava-flow intrusion in *Fragment II*. Here is a matt-black flood, as if the deluge of history had brought down the roof of Colvin's derelicted Scottish world-theatre.

1. Eric Stantner *Stranded Objects: Mourning, Memory and Film in Post-War Germany*, Ithaca; Cornell University Press, 1990, p.7.

Sarah Jones
Animating Nature

MORGAN FALCONER

The Park (II), 2002 *(left)*, Ilex (holly) (I), 2002 *(right)*

Over the past seven years the settings of Sarah Jones' photographs have followed a steady course from tightly closeted interiors to wilder exteriors. Some of her first settings were the most closeted of all: the *Consulting Room* pictures showed only psychoanalysts' couches; there was no suggestion of narrative, just the empty space above the pillow for the viewer's own projections. Later on came the *Mulberry Lodge* and *Francis Place* pictures, in which adolescent girls were arranged in a variety of dormant poses in the comfortable retreats of plush bourgeois homes. Following these came pictures of the gardens of those homes. Now she has begun a series which moves back and forth, between inside and outside, between homes and urban parkland.

Looking along the route Jones has taken, the new work might well be understood as a dialogue between two opposites, between authentic and constructed versions of the natural, but in fact it posits an uneasy equivalence between the two. Her parks suggest nature reserves, novel constructions halfway between being wild-flower gardens and real wilds. The nature which finds its way into Jones' domestic settings is hardly more cultured: effusive patterns cover everything from the fabrics which encase the furniture to the clothes which enwrap the figures; it is a nature that seems almost virulent in its spread, and choking in its hold. Jones doesn't only suggest parallels through her arrangement of the scenes, however, but also by the way in which she uses people and plants almost interchangeably as her central protagonists: in one picture, a young woman stands forward to animate the scene; in another, a woman reclines on a branch, blending into the backdrop; in another, the tree itself seems to step forward, holding the scene as potently as the women; and in another, a late season rose from a municipal garden offers itself as a figure every bit as expressive as the gesturing characters.

This series might be said to represent a new step in the composition of Jones' pictures, since in the past it was much easier to isolate her figures from her grounds; backdrops were employed more as stage sets for her characters than as their likely habitats. The women she has used in her new series are familiar with the parks they stand in, but in a wider sense their relationship to these new settings is still uncertain.

Perhaps it is because the rituals and observances of such activities as country rambling, or strolling in formal gardens, come freighted with a long history of meanings and social conventions, whereas the place of humanity within this new nature is yet to be clearly defined. Hence Jones' figures appear poised like theatrical protagonists, characters who can only mime their relationship to their surroundings, rather than speak it with certainty.

The ease with which theatrical metaphors can be applied to Jones' pictures is surely not accidental, since at the same time as she trained in visual art she also trained in theatre. Hence her practice engages with qualities of performance and rhetoric on many levels. Her pictures aren't exactly set like stages – after all, they depict parts of the natural world – but in the way they echo with moments from the history of art which have a similarity to contemporary interpretations of classic drama: Jones gives her figures poses and leaves them to, as she puts it, "fill them up", to reinterpret them with their own emotional truth. If there is indeed so much performance in Jones' pictures, however one might ask why they remain so silent. It is hardly that they seem distant, since the large formats of the prints do accommodate to the viewer's proportions. It is more a matter of their enunciative qualities as photographs. The absence of naturalistic realism is central to this: the scenes might be vivid with a profusion of observed detail but, as John Slyce has argued, the pictures are only 'performatively' real. Further-more, because the link between the literal world and the symbolic is left uncertain, her pictures take on an allegorical form. The poses of the women, the late blooming of the flower, the way the light animates the coiling branches of the tree: the images point to indeterminate meanings; and rather than the picture speaking unequivocally and self-evidently about a moment in the past, the scenes exist in open suspension, inhabiting a continual present tense. In this way Jones' pictures speak of the problematics of narrative in contemporary image-making; they show how the old conventions which wedded social life to pictorial iconography have fallen away. But in their sheer presence as images, their poise and expressive power, the photographs bear witness to the continuing need to represent the world.

John Askew
Flower

SIMON MORRISSEY

In John Askew's series *Flower* there are five pairs of mirrored images, each depicting a simple, green-stemmed white bloom. The white campanula is framed closely against a white background. And every image is the same: the flowers have turned their backs on the camera and each other, their white petals almost indistinguishable from their surroundings. They are pictures of a flower in which the flower is almost not there at all.

It is this self-conscious evasion that immediately suggests Askew's images have a distinctly individual agenda. The simple device of depicting the flower with its head turned away from the viewer anthropomorphises the bloom in an unexpected way. In comparison to the long tradition of depicting flowers as sexualised objects – so explicit in Robert Mapplethorpe's work for example – Askew's *Flower* appears modest, even demure. Yet is has a palpable, silent strength.

Like all of Askew's work, *Flower* gestated over a protracted period of years. In this sense, the concept of time-lapse is fundamentally enshrined at the very heart of the artist's working method. Askew often realises his series through the editing, re-photographing or recontextualising of images he has taken up to 20 years earlier. Even when not working at such a remove from his images' moment of origin, Askew consciously delays closure, working and reworking the images in an attempt to dislocate them from their source.

This desire to stress the photograph as an autonomous object as distinct from its referent emerges from Askew's preoccupation with the perennial conflict between the tangibility of photography's promise to represent memory and its ultimate inability to do so. Through different devices he has attempted to emphasise the status of photography as a chimera born of an explicitly mechanical process, a false promise of preservation that plays on our emotional reflexes.

The universality of this emotional reflex is underlined by the very fact that, despite his work's agenda, Askew's series always begin with material with which he has a close personal association. The choice of the model from this series came from the artist's realisation that his most elemental idea of a flower was the campanulas which his father grew in his garden. The period of development of the series also coincided with a time of serious illness for his mother. Askew made hundreds of images of the campanulas, at first as a reassurance in the face of uncertainty. But even this deeply emotional association became the beginning of the process of dislocation. The repetition moved steadily from its original impulse towards a mechanical expression of the beauty promised by concealment.

As the series approached its final conclusion, the idea of the mechanical became as important as that of the beautiful. The coexistence of these two states renders the images doubly empty, conjoining the lack we feel in the face of both the mechanical and the beautiful. This position found its final expression in the act of creating the mirrored images, itself one final mechanical multiplication.

In conversation, Askew is fond of recounting a Jewish legend. The legend describes how each millennium God sends an angel to earth to deliver a message to his people. Preparation for the mission takes countless years, the journey itself is long and complicated. It is so arduous that most of the messengers get lost on the way to earth, and those who finally reach their destination have forgotten what it was they were supposed to say. Askew posits this as a metaphor for photography in general – the beautiful, magical messenger that is ultimately empty of the meaning we expect it to bring – but it is especially pertinent for his own work.

The painter Luc Tymans observed that pictures, if they are to have an effect, must have the tremendous intensity of silence. *Flower* manages to open a silent space which gives rise to a myriad of associations. *Flower* could easily be a meditation on beauty, on death and resurrection, or even on humankind's increasingly radical interventions in nature. But *Flower* is essentially a paradox. It suggests all of these things through their explicit absence. It is an expression of the fact that the photograph is not so much a repository of memory as a screen onto which we project associations in an attempt to fill its emptiness. It is the embodiment of photography's withholding in the face of our desire for meaning.

Erasmus Schroeter
Theatre of Light

ROY EXLEY

Komparsen Frau XXV, 2001

When the Leipzig photographer, Erasmus Schroeter, chooses a subject for his camera, that subject invariably undergoes a transformation process. There is always a sense of theatricality in this transformation, which is at its most pronounced in his new series, *Komparsen* ('bit-part player'). In this series of staged photographs, despite his abandonment of the theatrical lighting which has featured prominently in his previous work, theatricality continues to be referenced through his use of theatre extras or 'bit-part players', who here are allotted a kind of stardom. To recruit the women who appear in this series, Schroeter perused the extras catalogues of the Theatres of Saxony, choosing women from that age range between youth and middle age, whose looks could be described as average rather than striking or beautiful. The demeanour of 'stardom', which he bestows upon these women, through his staging of the images, is deliberately paradoxical. Here are women who, in their ordinariness, challenge the stereotype of the star. Missing are the professional makeovers, absent is the feline or languid pose, lacking is that aura or charisma of the star. Nevertheless, Schroeter is elevating these extras to that solo, central role that they have never experienced before.

The venue for Schroeter's photo-shoot of the female extras is The Agra, an abandoned agricultural showground at Markleeberg, near Leipzig, which was formerly a showpiece of the German Democratic Republic. This is now a dismal, desolate place, rife with all the signs and symptoms of neglect and dereliction, with peeling paint, rust-streaked cladding, graffiti, weed-choked paths and terraces, and bilious coloured walls. The surroundings clash harshly with the women's bright clothing, bringing a tangible sense of tension to the images. While highlighting its decay and neglect, these photographs also seem to herald a false revival

of the site, in a doomed attempt to afford it fresh credibility. Frequently thronged by crowds in its GDR days, The Agra is now deserted, leaving its empty stage to these women for each of whom this ersatz stardom becomes a solipsistic and poignant event.

The female extras in these scenes offer a wide range of permutations on the archetypal glamorous blonde. However, they all share an enigmatic air of anomie, as they stare past the camera lens into the distance. This strategy, which in turn distances them from the viewer, gives them an aura of untouchability. *Frau II* in particular seems to convey a demeanour of absent inaccessibility, a sense of detachment, a visage that rings more of melancholy than aloofness and conveys a mien of vulnerable fragility rather than effusive celebrity. *Frau I*, with her passable emulation of a movie star, seems to be waiting in vain for an imaginary welter of fans, her inner despair almost palpable as a vestigial sense of imminence collapses in upon itself. We seem to be caught between two worlds here, the world of the paparazzi who stalk and poach the gloss of celebrity, and that of the documentary photographer who vainly attempts to capture reality. This is certainly a different universe to that inhabited by the likes of the photographers Rankin or Juergen Teller.

Schroeter's early work was made while he was living in Leipzig as an East German citizen, under the regime of the GDR, when both resources and opportunities for the artist were severely limited. This early work was monochrome and principally portraiture or social documentary – any critique of the Communist system was not an option. Schroeter, like many former East German residents, was no stranger to the excesses of the Stasi. After he applied for an exit visa in order to work in West Germany, the Stasi confiscated his identity papers and replaced them with documents which branded him as an 'enemy of the state'. It is not surprising, therefore, that much of Schroeter's later work is a barely veiled critique of the failed ideologies that polarised millions of lives in East Germany for over 50 years.

In his series *Bunker*, Schroeter's photographs of Hitler's Atlantic Coast Bunkers around the coasts of Brittany and Normandy transform them from the dour and desolate concrete monoliths, which appear in Paul Virilio's book *Bunker Archaeology*, into alluring sculptural objects. His use of powerful theatrical-lighting rigs floods these structures with vividly colourful, seductive light, which has the effect of re-inventing them, of elevating them, so that they shed their austerity and assume a passive but spectacular beauty. As menacing as these structures appeared in the early 1940's – named *Atlantikwall by* Hitler, and guarding his newly occupied territories of France, Belgium, Netherlands and Denmark from attack by the Allies – they were soon to be seen as extravagant follies. They have now been neutralised by the ravages of time and the elements, and ultimately mollified here by Schroeter's process of beautification.

Like the Fauvists, Schroeter seems to be drunk on colour, and is not frightened to strive for hyperbole in his boldly colour-saturated images. Whereas he relied on powerful coloured lighting in his *Bunker* series, in *Komparsen* he has permeated the scenes with photographic floodlighting, exaggerating the brightness of the women's clothing, their bleached hair and the sickly coloured hues of the painted buildings. Unlike his early work in the GDR, these images could never be described as documentary. Not only are the photographs carefully staged, but the aggressive presence of colour lends them an 'otherness', a strangeness that overwhelms and obscures what might otherwise be the subject matter of these works, but in fact becomes merely the armature upon which colour can play. In his essay entitled *The Black Paintings*, the American painter, Ad Reinhardt suggests that "Colour is always trapped in some kind of physical activity or assertiveness of its own." It is this same 'physical activity' that projects the colour into the foreground in Schroeter's images, and its 'assertiveness' that infuses these otherwise prosaic scenes with its new-found but ultimately superficial vigour. In his *Phenomenology of Perception*, Maurice Merleau-Ponty states that, "The real colour of things persists beneath their appearances, as the background persists beneath the figure." It seems that Schroeter is raising this idea onto another level, as he urges the colours to take on a life of their own, to overwhelm the forms and surfaces of which they are an intrinsic part.

Schroeter's Komparsen images, with their strident 'in your face' demeanour, sit somewhere between the immediacy of Beat Streuli's *Everyday* series, snatched street shots of urban dwellers picked out, seemingly at random, from the crowd, and Philip-Lorca DiCorcia's *Hollywood* series, poignant staged shots of Los Angeles rent-boys, drug addicts and drifters which parody and undermine the superficial gloss that is Hollywood.

Komparsen is somewhat more complex, but puts one in mind of a now famous statement that Roland Barthes made in his book *Camera Lucida*. Barthes stated, after looking at an 1852 photograph of Napoleon's brother, that "I am looking at the eyes that looked at the emperor." We could equally claim, on looking at the *Komparsen* images, that "We are looking at the eyes that avoided the stare of the Stasi," and now, we revel in its demise.

Bunker #12

Bunker #17

Bunker #29

Philip-Lorca diCorcia
Heads

MARK DURDEN

Head #13

"At the time it was the height of the boom economy – Giuliani was getting away with everything and Disney was coming in. Times Square was becoming a massive example of globalisation, American style. I wanted to deal with some aspect of this new America that everyone seemed so proud of but that seemed to me to be sort of soulless and completely material."[1]

If the uniform blankness and vacant looks in Philip-Lorca diCorcia's compelling recent series *Heads* – face-on portraits of a diversity of unsuspecting passers-by, all taken at the same spot in Times Square with a powerful telephoto lens – might be seen to point to a soullessness beneath the American spectacle culture and accord with a long-standing tradition of representations of lone and lonely subjects in urban spaces, they are nevertheless animated by being given something of the gloss and glow of fashion photography. For, in order to take these pictures, diCorcia – an artist who also works within commercial photography – rigged up an overhead strobe on scaffolding in Times Square, which he then triggered as his unsuspecting passers-by walked over an X marked on the sidewalk, the X marking the point at which the flashes were aimed and the camera focused. Spot lit in this way, diCorcia's ordinary subjects are given a theatrical presence, and their images literally lifted out of the bustling crowds as every detail of the surrounding environment is blacked out.

This effect makes sense in relation to diCorcia's earlier reliance on the staged and controlled effects of tableau photography. In his photographs from the late 1970s he directed friends and family members in imagined scenarios of everyday life – lavishly closed worlds in which his protagonists played out psychological dramas in domestic settings. Peter Galassi succinctly described the characteristic of such works as "an art of deep feeling wrapped in the shimmering package of consumer culture".[2] In many senses, this tension between seductive gloss and emotive intensity characterises all of diCorcia's work, and is as typical of *Heads* as his first tableau series.

The recipient of a National Endowment for the Arts grant, diCorcia left his domestic and familiar settings, providing an interesting variant on the tradition of documentary photography. For his series *Hollywood*, 1990-92, he mixed tableau photography with documentary – having carefully prepared a location and scene, he approached men on the street to pose for him; the men were picked up along Santa Monica Boulevard, an area frequented by drifters, drug addicts and prostitutes. Ebbing sunlight and the glow of neon signs give aura and grace to his otherwise 'low' subjects, rekindling the fantasies associated with Hollywood's dream factory. The crepuscular lighting also gives a melancholic edge to the pictures; death, one comes to feel, is not far away for many of these youths. DiCorcia's hybrid mixing of the tableau with documentary effectively introduces into his photography both the elements of pathos and expressivity often lacking in the tableau and an allure and visual seduction often lacking in documentary. The dialectic between artifice and realism continues when diCorcia moves into the genre of street photography, setting up hidden flashes, which illuminate unsuspecting pedestrians in his pictures from various cities around the world. Consequently, while taken from life, the resulting series of images, *Streetwork*, 1993-1997, were edged with the derealizing cinematographic effect of the tableau.

Heads is a continuation of *Streetwork*, and is a project which involves him going closer to the subjects, albeit a proximity effected through a powerful magnifying lens and involving the photographer always remaining out of the sight of those photographed. DiCorcia's series of portraits, selected from thousands of photographs, presents certain types, differentiated in terms of age, ethnicity and economic status. Identity and difference for many is signalled through dress. The lighting from above tends to function to elevate and ennoble these people – it is a romanticising and idealising light recalling Nadar's famous portraits of his bohemian friends. However, not all the subjects are lit in the same way, especially when two people happen to be caught in frame; in such pictures the sense of uniformly dignifying portraiture is upset.

The systematic and intrusive method in the making of diCorcia's portraits testifies to a process of anonymity and disengagement which breaks with traditional expectations of the portrait. Conventionally, the portrait sets up an expectancy about the revelation of identity, a disclosure of subjectivity, and a sense of the person portrayed. Traditional portraiture also entails some interaction between portrayer and portrayed. What is unsettling about diCorcia's pictures is that they are bereft of any sense of interiority and interaction. His remain fundamentally unresponsive subjects, captured in their ultimate otherness, completely unaware of being pictured. They appear to be elsewhere, distracted, absorbed in their own thoughts, cares and worries. And on the occasions when they appear to look to the camera they are seeing nothing.

In a fascinating recent essay on a series of portraits similar to diCorcia's, taken surreptitiously on the Paris metro by Luc Delahaye, Jean Baudrillard says that what is captured "isn't exactly the Other but what remains of the Other when he, the photographer, isn't there: the ill-assorted gazes of people who see nothing; who are, most importantly, not looking at one another, obsessed as they are with protecting their own symbolic space."[3] He develops an argument about these portraits and this photography being bereft of any forced signification – the antithesis of much photography which "short-circuits the otherness of the object... by mediating it through an idea of one sort or another." Baudrillard gives us the example of contemporary photography condemned in the name of realism and testimony "to photograph victims as such, the dead as such, the poverty-stricken as such." Delahaye's photography interests Baudrillard because it is seen as part of "an exaltation of what the camera sees in its pure self-evidence, without intercession, concession or embellishment." Such portraits, bereft of any signs of response, exchange and interaction, show "that which is of the order of the inhuman in us."

But as much as one can understand the logic of Baudrillard's thesis, one can never fully respond to diCorcia's portraits in this extreme way. Compared to Delahaye's mass of black-and-white pictures, diCorcia's selective series of colour life-sized portraits are much more embellished and rich. Clarity of image and the theatricalising illumination gives each one of his subjects a heightened presence and legibility.

In his introductory essay to the book of diCorcia's portraits, Luc Sante picks out the recurrence of furrowed brows and reads the pictures in terms of urban alienation and isolation. He also proposes that the most private look is now the most public look. Alone and unseen among the crowds there is no need to hide your feelings. The mask is down. While heightened and melodramatic, diCorcia's pictures are, for Sante, "of the starkest realism".[4]

The idea of unmasking was integral to Walker Evans' *Many Are Called*, a collection of portraits taken with a hidden camera of fellow passengers on the Manhattan subways in 1938. An "angry protest – not social, but aesthetic – against posed portraiture" was how Evans described such pictures.[5] His direct and raw anonymous urban portraits were meant as an authentic counterpoint to the fakery and theatre of the commercial portraiture of the likes of Beaton, Karsh and Steichen. The subway portraits are testimonials to estrangement, both through Evans' distance from the strangers whose portraits he steals and these people's own psychological remoteness from one another, despite their physical proximity on the subway. Like Delahaye's contemporary versions, Evans' pictures are closer to Baudrillard's thesis. Evans' subway portraits, in minimising his own artistic presence, are also crucial to the photographer's distinctive modernist sensibility. In this series he set out to achieve what he later described as the "ultimate purity" of the "record method."[6] They extend his disengaged and detached aesthetic, already a discernible characteristic of his formal and cool depictions of poor tenant farmer families of the American South taken a few years earlier.

DiCorcia's hybrid portraits, while they look back to Evans' unposed subway portraits, are embellished with a cinematic look. If Evans believed his stolen portraits caught his subjects unmasked, without a conscious presentation of self, diCorcia's subjects remain masked in the sense that, for all the individualising contingent details, they remain generic, reduced and abstracted to various types. The project may involve processes out of strict authorial control, but the lighting and selection of the final pictures brings them back into control and offsets the uneasy sense of otherness and indifference which is integral to the way the pictures were made. The rawness of Evans' (and Delahaye's) subway pictures is tamed and diCorcia's nameless subjects have more the appearance of choreographed actors adopting particular social roles and positions. Such an effect makes the pictures very palatable and stylish. Filtered through fiction and fantasy, the Other is made familiar.

1. Quote taken from Jorge Blanco's article 'Head On: Philip-Lorca diCorcia' in *Planet*, Issue Zero, Summer 2001, p.44.

2. Peter Galassi in The Museum of Modern Art, *Philip-Lorca diCorcia*, New York, 1995, p11.

3. See Jean Baudrillard's 'Poetic Transference of Situation' in *L'Autre: Luc Delahaye*, Phaidon: London, 1999, n.p. All following quotes from this essay.

4. Luc Sante in *Philip-Lorca diCorcia, Heads*, New York and Germany, Steidl Box Pace/Macgill Gallery, New York, 2001, n.p.

5. Quoted in Mia Felman's essay 'Notes from the Underground: The Subway Portraits' in Maria Morris Hambourg et al. *Walker Evans*, The Metropolitan Museum of Art, New York, 2000, p.108.

6. Ibid., p.114.

Head #13

William Eggleston
Hayward Gallery, London

JEREMY MILLAR

Untitled, (Mississippi) 1970

One of the great stories by that great American writer Raymond Carver is entitled 'What we talk about when we talk about love'. Now, one might assume that what we talk about when we talk about love is, indeed, love, yet Carver did not call his story, simply, 'Love'. Instead, what we talk about when we talk about love is our feelings about love, our hesitancy, our ignorance, our convictions, our wishes, our uncertainties when confronted by something profound and overwhelming. This is how I feel when confronted by the photographs of William Eggleston, profound and overwhelming as they are. This is what we talk about when we talk about William Eggleston.

Walking around this exhibition, or looking through the accompanying publication, one cannot help but be struck by the audacious simplicity of the work. Perhaps Eggleston is better because he looks so much harder, one thinks, yet was there ever a person who looked so easily, who made looking look so easy? I doubt it. Bare twigs against a wall seem to trace the graceful arcing trajectories of the red butterfly leaves at their end; the red 'L' of a girder at a drive-in restaurant, a slick of a stainless steel tray and the black spots of gum on the asphalt, like a spreading malignancy; the businessman caught amongst the flat planes of his hotel room, a glass in his hand, his suitcase open, like he has just checked in yet is contemplating other ways in which he might check out. One can even imagine Eggleston drawn to the white dress hanging in the sunlight just as the wasps crawling across its surface were, yet not for him their indecision, their hesitant crawl, but rather just one exposure, as always, and presented as is.

The 'everyday' is Eggleston's great subject, indeed is photography's great subject. Yes, there was an emerging aesthetic of the everyday in the late 18th and early 19th centuries, with Archibald Alison claiming that the beautiful and the sublime are "almost constantly before us", or Wordsworth finding paradise "a simple product of the common day", yet it was only with the development of photography that this aesthetic approached its true potential. Fox Talbot recognised this immediately, remarking that, "A painter's eye will often be arrested where ordinary people see nothing remarkable. A casual gleam of sunshine, or a shadow thrown across a path, a time-withered oak, or a moss-covered stone may awaken a train of thoughts and feelings, and picturesque imaginings." One might find all of these things in this exhibition, yet Eggleston seems little interested in demonstrating the difference between his vision and that of 'ordinary people'. One feels there is remarkably little ego in Eggleston's photographs, no inviolate belief in the power of his own artistic sensibility to allow the commonplace to reveal its transcendental beauty without recourse to any significant intervention. We might think we are party, once more, to the 'transfiguration of the commonplace', yet for Eggleston this seems unnecessary. Why bother? What's banal here? People? Nature? The world we're creating or that which we're destroying? *Banal?* It is only within the everyday that everything finds its real significance, he seems to say, that everything *is* everyday and significant. Just look at the photograph taken at a family funeral in 1970. Dead leaves shroud the ground upon which two men stand, one black, one white, their jackets white and black. Just behind them a car, its door open and its driver hiding beneath the reflected sky; further back is water, flat and brown now yet the scene of tragedy in the past. And they stand, these men, different in their different ways, standing there no doubt for different reasons, but they stand together nonetheless, stand the same way, amongst the leaves and wire, bags and cans, and here is compassion and duty, habit and love. Looking here, now, I feel it almost impossible to conceive how such a photograph might be taken, yet perhaps more strongly, I feel it almost impossible to conceive that such a photograph might not have been taken, that, in a sense, it seems impossible that this photograph could not exist. Like all great art it has a sense of the inevitable about it. It is the picture I would carry, running, from any burning museum.

There are a number of things that are often claimed of Eggleston – that his was the first exhibition of colour photographs at MoMA, or the first exhibition of colour photographs in a New York museum, or even, extraordinarily, by the Hayward itself, that his was the first ever exhibition of colour photographs. All are wrong, and all miss the point. More important is that nobody took better photographs before him, and nobody has taken better photographs since. Perhaps that is all there is to talk about.

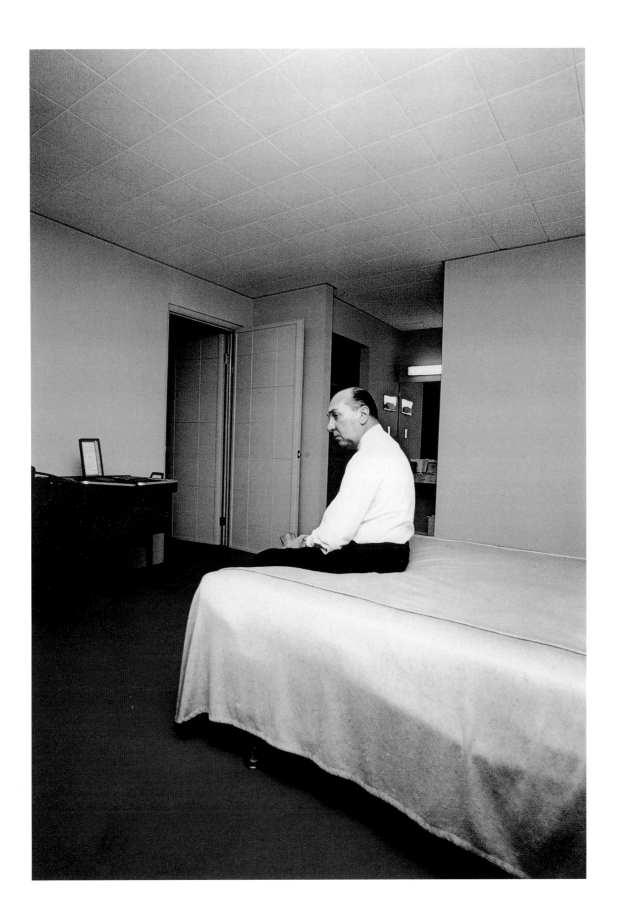

Untitled (Huntsville, Alabama) 1969-70

Hill and Adamson: Facing the Light
Scottish National Portrait Gallery, Edinburgh

AMANDA HOPKINSON

'Calotype' is simply the Greek term for 'beautiful print'. Two hundred of these early photographic images from the 1840s have attracted over 25,000 visitors since this exhibition opened in May 2002. Drawn from a national collection of some 5,000 plate glass negatives of the pioneering photographers Hill and Adamson – their names, along with that of Daguerre in France and Fox Talbot in England, synonymous with the 'invention' of photography – and housed in Scotland's National Portrait Gallery, they comprise not only some of the most beautiful works of art on display anywhere, but also the first social documentary of a living local community photographed anywhere at any time.

Its excavation and presentation has been a dedicated labour of love on the part of senior curator Sara Stevenson, who compiled the exhibition and provided the catalogue. But the concept originated in David Octavius Hill's artistic practice, which combined a love of natural beauty with a desire to record events of social importance. Many of these are now relegated to the realms of largely forgotten or ignored local history. Events of such contemporary magnitude as the Disruption of the Church of Scotland are now hardly terms to conjure with. Yet it was one of the great moral issues of its day and, or so it seemed, in the first millennia of Christianity; for the devolution of pastors from the state protection left nearly all without either living or income, deliberately adrift and homeless among their flock over an issue of principle. At its heart the matter was less about nationalism than about how to live as a Christian – within the Establishment or without, according to the light of individual conscience – and it spurred Hill to spend three years in making calotype portraits of those men he clearly regarded as pilgrims in the mould of Bunyan's Christian and to devoting a further 23 years to painting a record of the congregation of ministers seceding to form a Free Church.

Whether it was the greater likeness that could be achieved or the lesser time the process required, Hill was clearly satisfied with the series of portraits that open this exhibition. What is of interest to a present-day viewer is the social context these calotypes provide. Portraits in the main of devout men reduced to living in straitened circumstances that often resemble the rural Middle Ages more than the second Industrial Revolution are a necessary counterpart to the grand oil painting of the Disruption now hanging in the Free Church in Edinburgh.

The fascination lies in the detail, as much technical as social. Preachers were recorded in the out of doors, where the heavy box camera with its massive brass lens could be set up, which lends a valid air of a church brought to the people, made accessible by not being immured within ecclesiastical architecture. The mechanical props used to sustain the Free Church's leader Dr. Thomas Chalmers' arms raised in dramatic emphasis – or the human props used to steady subjects obliged to pose for extended periods – contrast with such unexpected expressions as the warm smile on the Rev.Hugh Mackay MacKenzie's face. The Rev. Dr. Henry Duncan has clearly brought his smart Regency striped armchair into exile, and is seated outdoors in the Scottish weather, as if this were the most natural place to be while devising an early version of Trustees' Savings Banks. And the Rev. John Jaffray has chosen to share a joint portrait with Dhanjiobai Nauroji, in full traditional Parsee clothing including a dervish's head-dress, to demonstrate the force of righteous persuasion upon this recent convert and minister.

The key to these beautiful curiosities lies in the original oil of the Disruption. In it are included painted portraits of Hill himself, with a sketchbook, and Robert Adamson, his photography tutor and facilitator, partly submerged beneath the black cloth draping his camera. David Brewster, physicist and inventor of versions of the kaleidoscope and stereoscope, was responsible for introducing the two men, an occasion he recorded in a letter to Fox Talbot. "I got hold of the Artist [Hill], shewed him the Calotype, & the immense advantage he might derive from it in getting likenesses of all the principal characters before they dispersed to their respective homes. He was at first incredulous, but went to Mr. Adamson, and arranged with him the preliminaries for getting all the necessary Portraits. They have succeeded beyond their most sanguine expectations... "

Such success led to a partnership that was to establish photography as far more than merely the medium of providing accurate working likenesses, or even dramatic portraits. Soon Hill, basing his work on Adamson's technical skills, determined on photography as his medium of choice in capturing the ambitions that had earlier moved him as an artist. The son of a bookseller, his literary and bucolic interests had already led him to provide illustrations for both Wordsworth and Burns, and to undertake such projects as compiling a set of lithographs of the new Glasgow & Garnkirk Railway. Photography suddenly opened new possibilities in recording both traditional ways of life lest they disappear, and of celebrating the many innovations that were transforming major Scottish cities.

In Edinburgh alone, Hill and Adamson worked together on such novel undertakings as the Scott Monument, begun in 1840. In case contemporary viewers should get the idea that documenting novelties bore any resemblance to present-day press photography we should bear in mind that Hill and Adamson spent two years (1843-45), much of it atop the roof of the Royal Institution, angling their cameras to take the 'wedding-cake' layers of the monument as they mounted on an edifice Gladstone described as 'elaborate and very lofty', and Ruskin puzzlingly contrasted as 'a small vulgar Gothic steeple'. True to style, however, the reportage included some fine shots of stonemasons working outdoors in startling sunlight, apparently carving angels' wings, and of the finished monument shown to scale with the grandeur of the castle behind and a lamp-post and a posed group of Sunday walkers in the foreground.

Other series included further homage to Sir Walter Scott via pictures of costumed characters drawn from the Waverley novels at Lord Cockburn's neo-baronial haunt, Bonaly Tower, but also of the Gordon Highlanders, stationed at Edinburgh Castle during 1846. Intended as part of a series entitled Edinburgh Old and New, this extensive sequence is perhaps the most daring there is of the period, for the amount of movement permitted. Gone are the strictures of props and braces placed on the earlier portraits, the poses with downcast eyes, folded hands or arms akimbo. Here the soldiers are clearly on active service, cleaning their gun-barrels, mounting their canon and rehearsing the band. Hill and Adamson brilliantly contrast the etched outlines of colour in even their tartan socks with the blur of motion essential to the business of troops on the move.

Perhaps the most cherished of all of the many series the pair created during their four short years of working together is that of the Newhaven fishing community. Once again they were led towards it at least partially in consequence of the great Disruption. And once again, the Rev. Thomas Chalmers was a major influence. His work in attempting to keep a community together – rather than allowing Highland clearances and rural poverty to lead only to dispersal among the slums of overgrown cities – was modelled in the nearby fishing port of Newhaven. Together Hill and Adamson compiled a large set of prints advertised, in their list of 1844, as showing The Fishermen and Women of the Firth of Forth. Again, their knowledge and respect of and for the community is evident in the detail: they followed many of the individuals through their working days, acknowledging each by name and description.

Like members of other classes, these people conformed to virtual uniforms: the women wore printed striped calico, rather like mattress ticking, with copious aprons, shawls and sun-bonnets (or caps, if married). These fishwives are shown carting great creels of fish, selling it door-to-door or preparing it for market, and seeing to the repair of both nets and baskets. Surprisingly, at least some were sufficiently literate to be shown reading aloud from the 'penny post', an increasingly vital means of communication with men fishing ever further afield. The men, meanwhile, are dressed either in knee breeches or in white mariners' trousers, all suitably stained as befits sailors whose work is never done, and an astonishing variety of hats, ranging from the sou'wester to the stovepipe. Children also, were never too young to find employment in Newhaven, and several shots show groups of girls or boys huddled (often giggling) on or under boats. One boy captioned

simply as 'King Fisher', with the alternative title 'His Faither's Breeks' (for the baggy cutdowns he wears, along with an ill-fitting shirt and tam-o'-shanter) is deemed to have been an orphan, for being alone in having no name of his own.

The whole presents the dignity of labour in the round: dirty and arduous, but also as a feat of personal commitment and a source of social support. Chalmers was to use the fishing community as his model for closing an entire district of Glasgow to outside poor relief, in order to regenerate some of the old spirit of neighbourliness and mutual concern even within the new city slums. Travel photographers would soon venture far afield to document extravagantly exotic cultures, while the Pictorialists would sentimentalise rural poverty and early death. Yet even when documenting the decline of such cities as St. Andrews, the abandon of Highland villages, or the roots of poverty new and old, Hill and Adamson avoided the sensational and the sentimental, grounding themselves in their own country and culture.

Yet mortality is never far from many of their stories. It is implicit in such series as that on the Gordon Highlanders, fresh home from the wars, and in the dangers of life at sea. The highly stylised sidelit portrait of the fishwife Elizabeth Johnstone Hall also had alternate captions. While one described her as 'A Newhaven Beauty', the other simply quotes her statement 'It's no fish ye're buying it's men's lives.' Of the many Scottish graveyard tales, there are few more heart-rending than that of Greyfriars cemetery (where little dog Bobby famously went daily to wait at the tomb of his dead guardian) or more matter-of-fact than the portraits of grave-diggers going about their business of burial. A less maudlin, more humorous route was taken with the first known (staged) depiction of a massive hangover (called, naturally enough, 'The Morning After', following the jollity of 'Edinburgh Ale'), which are also campaigning images for Dr. Miller's temperance movement.

Mortality was to impinge directly and far too soon upon the working partnership. In 1848, after a wasting illness, Robert Adamson died, back in St. Andrews. Observing that "Poor Adamson has not left his like in the arts in which he was so modest," Hill also abandoned photography and returned to painting. Four short years of collaboration, one testament to which has to be the natural wonder of 'The Faerie Tree', one of the last and most beautiful images the pair took together. Taken in Colinton woods in the grounds of Lord Dumferline's estate, the light shimmers through the branches in ethereal fantasy. Hill and Adamson's subjects may have had to have been taken 'Facing the Light', to allow maximum illumination of their characteristic features: the tree allows a unique experience of translucence.

Hill was to pay homage to Adamson for calotypes "first raising the process to the rank of a Fine Art, or rather to that of one of its most magical and potent auxiliaries." And Paul Strand acknowledged Hill's contribution with: "The results of Hill's experimenting have given us a series of amazing portraits... They remain the most extraordinary assertion of the possibility of the utterly personal control of a machine, a camera." This exhibition, the first that seriously pays overdue respect to a formative partnership that was to prove formative for the whole of photography, goes an important way towards linking the elaboration of beauty with acute social documentary. Happily, the archives still possess the potential for further explorations and exhibitions of a short but fertile collaboration which goes to the roots and the heart of the photographic tradition.

Photographs opposite: Group of 92nd Gordon Highlanders (left); Edinburgh Ale (centre); It's No fish ye're buying...(Newhaven) (right).

Simon Norfolk
Afghanistan

SHIRLEY READ

King Amanullah's Victory Arch built to celebrate the 1919 Independence from the British, Paghman, Kabul Province *(left)*;
Bullet-scarred apartment building and shops in the Karte Char district of Kabul *(right)*

Time and space are the subjects of Simon Norfolk's recent work *Afghanistan: Chronotopia* which has won the European Publishers Award for Photography 2002. A chronotope is a word used by Soviet intellectual Mikhail Bakhtin to describe a landscape which allows simultaneous movement through time and space, and it is the layering of time and space that Norfolk has detailed in this work, describing it as an archaeology of almost 25 years of devastation within Afghanistan.

The Afghanistan he depicts seems stilled, trapped in its desolation, as if man has played out some truly terrible fate on a stage in a long-forgotten theatre. This is a land outside time and there is little in these apparently peaceful images to remind us of what we know of 21st Century warfare. US military tents at Bagram airbase could have been photographed by Roger Fenton in the Crimea. The litter of abandoned and rusting armaments rotting gently into the earth appears ancient. These could be images from a modern Pompeii, a lost place preserved after some gigantic calamity and dug up out of the past. What remains is a seemingly timeless pastoral landscape – still figures watch their grazing herds as they have through the centuries; the ruins of buildings in western Kabul appear to be returning to the sand; even the frescoes in the empty ruin of the Presidential swimming pool are more Roman than contemporary.

Space too appears solidified in what Norfolk refers to as a "museum of the archaeology of war". Evidence of the wars and invasions of the last decades lies in layers, each separately identifiable but seemingly frozen; frozen perhaps by the quality of the light – clear, suffusing, luminescent – speaking of the beginning or end of time and perhaps by the staggering scale of the landscape. This is a place which makes human activity seem unimportant, the vast landscapes apparently deserted, emptied of people by war. Other than shepherds or goat herds, only the occasional wanderer, clutching the inexplicable relics of a lost way of life – a fighting bird in a cage or a bunch of bright balloons – is to be seen in this post-apocalyptic desert. The only movement is that of a boy with his sheep, but behind him a ruined building looms, precariously close to engulfing them if it were to collapse.

Norfolk is a landscape photographer who works with landscapes of war and, in the tradition of Richard Misrach and Sophie Ristelhueber, deals with the traces and the aftermath of military action in the desert landscape, noting the strange beauty of war. His images record the eerie resemblance of tail fins of mortar rounds to the flowers of desert cactus, the way a tank track looks like a sloughed-off snakeskin, cluster bombs and canon casings which resemble stones and dried seed pods.

The beauty of these images of war and the play on the aesthetics of devastation is deeply disturbing. Norfolk has documented the gutted Presidential palace at Darulaman, scarred government buildings and the damaged victory arch at Paghman, all lit by an unearthly light. He refers to painters Claude Lorraine and Caspar David Freidrich as precedents for these photographs of the ruins of once great buildings, caught momentarily in the light as the greatness of human achievement faded leaving only the power of God. Similarly there is an echo of the scale of Ansel Adams' landscapes in which human achievements seem short-lived and puny before the enduring power of nature.

However, Norfolk constantly reminds us that this is a human tragedy. One of the things which make this work particularly remarkable is that most of it was made in December 2001 when Afghanistan was under attack from the West. To operate in a war zone with a large format camera is an act of courage or foolhardiness, depending on your point of view, but to do so with the same characteristic detachment that Norfolk brought to his previous work on sites of genocide is extraordinary, and, in fact, illusory. These apparently quiet tableaux of a post-apocalyptic landscape reverberate with an intense energy of information and anger.

Norfolk is above all a storyteller, and his images overflow with a sense of stories yet to be told and the now stilled traces of human activity. They are memorials to the people who used the empty roads and ruined buildings and whose ingenuity made use of wrecked Russian tanks for footings for temporary bridges. Each photograph is marked by this absence. This is a work of mourning.

Contributors

Artists

Erasmus Schroeter
Komparsen Series, 2000-2001
C-prints/Diasec
120 x 150 cm
Erasmus Schroeter is based in Leipzig and his work has been shown internationally. Recent exhibitions include *Theatre of the Unseen*, 13 November - 23 December 2002 at UH-Galleries, University of Hertfordshire, Hatfield, and 16 January - 1 March 2003 at Focal Point Gallery, Southend-on-Sea ; *Etats de Guerre*, 11 November - 1 December 2002, Centre Rhénan de la photographie, Strasbourg, France; *Komparsen, Neue Fotogafien*, 27 June - 8 August 2003 at Kunstverein Marburg, Germany.

Philip-Lorca diCorcia
Heads, 2000
C-Type, Fuji Crystal Archive
48 x 60 inches
Courtesy Pace/MacGill Gallery, New York
The book *heads* by Philip-Lorca diCorcia was published by SteidlBoxPacemacgill, 2001 (ISBN 3-88243-441-4), in conjunction with the exhibition of the same title at PaceWildenstein Chelsea, New York, 6 September to 13 October, 2001. Philip-Lorca diCorcia was a finalist in the Citigroup Private Bank Photography Prize, at the Photographers' Gallery, London, February/March 2002.

Victor Burgin
Watergate, 2000
Listen to Britain, 2002
Video installations with sound
Courtesy Christine Burgin Gallery, New York
Watergate was commissioned by the Corcoran Museum of Art, Washington, D.C., and first shown in the context of the 2000-01 Corcoran Biennial. The installation is at Matt's Gallery, London, 4 October to 1 December, 2002. *Listen to Britain* was commissioned by Arnolfini, Bristol, and shown in a retrospective of the artist's work from 21 September - 17 November 2002.
These works are included in the book *Relocating: Victor Burgin*, with essays by Catsou Roberts, Stephen Bann, Peter Osborne and Françoise Parfait, published by August Media/Arnolfini (ISBN 1-902854-19-5).

Simon Norfolk
Afghanistan, 2002
Pigment giclee prints
54 x 44 inches
Simon Norfolk won the The European Publishers' Award for Photography 2002, with his work on Afghanistan, resulting in publication of a book by five publishers, in five languages in five countries – *Afghanistan: Chronotopia* by Simon Norfolk published by Dewi Lewis Publishing (ISBN 1-899235-54-X).
An exhibition is touring internationally, including Gallery f.OTO, Bosnia Herzegovina, 27 August - 15 September 2002; Deutches Architektur Museum, Frankfurt, 23 October - 23 November 2002; Florence Photography Festival, October/November 2002; Neue Galerie, Graz, Austria, during Graz 2003 European City of Culture, 12 January to 26 March 2003.

John Askew
Flower
C-type photographs
24 x 20 inches
John Askew recently completed an MA in Fine Art at Goldsmiths College. He lives and works in London where is is currently recipient of a *Fire Station* Residency (2002-2005).

Susan Hiller
From India to the Planet Mars, 1998
Photographic negatives mounted on light boxes
20 x 30 inches
Courtesy Gagosian Gallery, London
From India to the Planet Mars comprises a collection of various automatic writings and drawings from artists, students, psychiatric patients, poets, etc. The series will be exhibited in the group exhibition *Apparition: The Action of Appearing*, at Arnolfini, Bristol, 30 November 2002 - 9 February 2003.

Calum Colvin
Ossian: Fragments of Ancient Poetry, 2002
Digital prints on canvas, 125 x 100 cm
The exhibition *Ossian: Fragments of Ancient Poetry* is at the Scottish National Portrait Gallery, 3 October 2002 to 9 February 2003; Inverness Museum and Art Gallery, 15 February - 15 March 2003; Swanson Gallery, Caithness, 21 March - 19 April 2003; An Tuireann, Isle of Skye, May/June 2003; St Fergus Gallery, Caithness, June/July 2003 and Iona Gallery, Kingussie, August/September 2003. A catalogue, with an essay by Tom Normand, is published by the National Galleries of Scotland (ISBN 1-903278-35-X).

Anne Kathrin Greiner
Disciplined Spaces: Aspects of 3 German Schools
C-type prints, 50 x 40 cm
Anne Kathrin Greiner was born in Germany and graduated from the BA Photography, Film and Imaging Course at Napier University, Edinburgh, in 2002. For her major project, she produced the series *Disciplined Spaces,* which explores the architecture of educational institutions by photographing in the three schools in Germany in which she had studied from the ages of seven to 19. In her photographs Greiner invokes personal memories of those institutions.

Minka Jakerson
The Yearning Room
Film stills/C-type prints, 50 x 40 cm
Minka Jakerson was born in Sweden and studied photography and film at Edinburgh College of Art, graduating in 2002. *The Yearning Room* is a film installation presented on two screens, which explores the notion of romance as a cultural institution in which our central measure of self-being is being desired by someone else.

Jung Lee
Clubgenki Series, 2002
C-type prints, 50 x 60 cm
Jung Lee was born in Seoul, South Korea, and lives and works in London. She graduated from the BA (Hons) Editorial & Advertising Photography at Kent Institute of Art & Design in 2002. Her work explores Western perception of Oriental women and, after working with artificially staged images, Lee became a member of Clubgenki in central London, where Western men and Oriental girls get together every Friday night.The series consists of 11 images, forming a filmic sequence.

Sarah Jones
C-type prints on aluminium, 150 x 150 cm
Courtesy Maureen Paley Interim Art, London
Sarah Jones' recent solo exhibitions include Maureen Paley Interim Art, London, 28 October - 24 November 2002; Anton Kern Gallery, New York, and le Consortium Dijon. Her work has been part of *No World Without You, Reflections of Identity in New British Art,* Herzliya Museum of Art, Tel Aviv, and *Representing Britain*, Tate Britain. She can also be seen in *Die Wohltat der Kunst: Post Feministische Positionen der 90er Jahre aus der Sammlung Goetz,* Staatliche Kunstalle, Baden-Baden until 10 November and will be included in *Painting Pictures,* Kunst-museum, Wolfsburg, from 1 March - 1 June 2003.

Martina Mullaney
Turn In
Lamda prints on aluminium, 48 x 48 inches
Martina Mullaney is an Irish artist currently living and working in Newport, South Wales, who studied Documentary Photography at the School of Art, Media and Design, UWCN. She has produced a series of photographic works in the environment of hostels and night shelters, which respond metaphorically to notions of isolation and remoteness.
The large-scale photographs have been organised into an exhibition by Ffotogallery, Cardiff, and presented in 20 illuminated Adshel poster sites on bus shelters throughout the city during late September/early October 2002.

Salvatore Arancio
The Ballroom Dancers, 2001
C-type prints, 50.8 x 76.2 cm
Salvatore Arancio was born in Italy and is a graduate of the BA Photography Course at London College of Printing (2001). His portraits of ballroom dancers at international dance competitions focus on competitors entering the Latin dances section. Arancio's interest arose from how the entrants, from diverse locations, all appear to have adopted a universal 'Latin' look.

Paul Thomas
Sauna
A series of 30 C-type prints, 60 x 48 inches
Paul Thomas graduated from the BA Editorial Photography Course at the University of Brighton in 2002. His series *Sauna* is the first part of a trilogy of investigations into sexually charged spaces, and deal with both male sexual identity and specifically constructed interiors.

Gina Glover
Outside Time
C-type Pinhole Photographs, 40 x 40 cm
Gina Glover is a freelance photographic artist and founder/director of Fotofusion Photography Centre in London, where she jointly curates the gallery and education programme. Her early work ranged from documentary photography to the exploration of family life. She currently focuses on our relationship with nature and inner struggles to make sense of the world. Her work has been recently exhibited at the Tom Blau Gallery in London, Trace in Weymouth, Huddersfield Art Gallery, Bexhill Costume and Natural History Museum, and her public artwork shown at the Central Middlesex Hospital in London. She is currently Photographic Artist in Residence in the Genetics Department of Guys Hospital in London.

Writers

Mark Durden is Reader in History and Theory of Photography at the University of Derby.

Stella Santacatterina is a curator, writer and freelance lecturer based in London.

David Alan Mellor is an art historian and curator and teaches at the University of Sussex.

Morgan Falconer is a freelance journalist. his writing has appeared in *Art Review, The Royal Academy Magazine* and *Untitled*.

Simon Morrissey is a critic and independent curator based in London.

Roy Exley is a writer, critic and curator who writes regularly for *Contemporary Visual Art* and *Untitled*.

Jeremy Millar is an artist and curator, and Director of the Brighton Photo Biennial 2003.

Amanda Hopkinson is a writer and is Senior Research Fellow in the School of Journalism, the University of Wales, Cardiff.

Shirley Read is an independent curator currently working in the Camera Press archive to produce exhibitions of vintage prints for the Tom Blau Gallery.

Celebrating 30 Years

Julie Henry

7 December 2002 - 1 February 2003

Comission in collaboration with Film and Video Umbrella

Julie Henry's photographic and video works spotlight the all-too-human profiles of frequently overlooked protagonists - the amateur talent show contestant, the video game wizkid, the local pub hotshot, the neighbourhood 'face' - in a series of still and moving image works that are as stark and compelling as they are disarming and affectionate.

Illustration of Life   **Max Kandhola**

Saturday 5 April to 31 May 2003

An Impressions Gallery Touring Show, in partnership with Light Works USA and supported by Nottingham Trent University

In our unpredictable world there is one certainty we can always rely on, yet death, when it comes is never easy. Max Kandhola's astonishingly beautiful photographs, show the brief moment just before and just after the death of his father, and represent the struggle to understand the process of dying.

Impressions Gallery
29 Castlegate
York YO1 9RN

Tel 01904 654724   Fax 01904 651509
enquiries@impressions-gallery.com
www.impressions-gallery.com

Opening Hours
Monday to Saturday
10.00am - 6.00pm

Yorkshire Arts   CITY OF YORK COUNCIL   THE ARTS COUNCIL OF ENGLAND

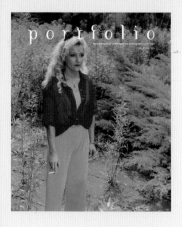

portfolio

the catalogue of contemporary photography in britain

PORTFOLIO is the best way to keep informed about the most innovative photographic art created and shown in Britain. Published in June and December each year, PORTFOLIO combines the current reviews and contemporary interests of a magazine with the quality reproductions and detailed information of an exhibition catalogue.

Past issues have featured the work of established photographic artists with in-depth essays and lively reviews from esteemed writers and curators. Back issues can be obtained individually or in a money-saving set of the ten most recent catalogues.

Visit our website at www.portfoliocatalogue.com

subscriptions

UK: Individuals – £34 for 4 issues / £18 for 2 issues Institutions, Libraries and Colleges – £45 for 4 issues / £25 for 2 issues
EUROPE – £45 for 4 issues / £25 for 2 issues WORLDWIDE – £55 for 4 issues / £30 for 2 issues

☐ Please start my (4 issue/2 issue) *(please indicate)* subscription to Portfolio with Number 37 (June 2003)

☐ Please send me back issue numbers *(please indicate)* _____ 11.50 (UK) £12.50 (Europe) £15.00 (Worldwide)

☐ Please send me a set of ten back issues (Numbers 26 – 35) at £79 (UK) £89 (Europe) £112 (Worldwide)

☐ I enclose a (Sterling) cheque (made payable to PORTFOLIO) for £ _____

☐ Or debit my Access/Visa/Mastercard *(delete as applicable)* [ ][ ][ ][ ][ ][ ][ ][ ][ ][ ][ ][ ][ ][ ][ ][ ] Expiry Date

Name _____

Signed _____

Address _____

Postcode _____

Return to PORTFOLIO, 43 Candlemaker Row, Edinburgh, EH1 2QB Scotland UK
Tel (44) 0131 220 1911 Fax (44) 0131 226 4287 Email info@portfoliocatalogue.com www.portfoliocatalogue.com